A practical guide for living happily in the most challenging times of your life.

BE A MONK

CHETAN PRABHAKAR

First Published in November 2021

ISBN: 978-93-5472-424-4

BLUEROSE PUBLISHERS

www.bluerosepublishers.com

info@bluerosepublishers.com

+91 8882 898 898

Cover Design:

Vanshika

Typographic Design:

Namrata Saini

Distributed by: BlueRose, Amazon, Flipkart, Shopclues

I am thankful, grateful and indebted to all the known and unknown Buddhas, Mystics, Spiritual Masters, Saints, Prophets, Yogis, Rishis, Sufis, Gods and Goddesses of the Universe for guiding me directly or indirectly on the path of spirituality and helping me to manifest this book.

I recommend the readers to read this book in 22 days as this book has 22 chapters and every chapter has its own unique message, understanding of which will lead the reader to a higher state of consciousness and ultimately, true happiness and eternal bliss. Earlier, I wanted to name this book 'Awakening to True Happiness', however, the name 'Be a Monk' seemed more appropriate considering that this book provides an insight into the practise of Right Mindfulness which is a basic practise recommended by the Buddha to Monks. By way of this book, I earnestly wish the readers to reach a state of equanimity, true happiness and eternal bliss. Hope this book helps you to reach that state of consciousness and your life is transformed.

Special thanks to my parents Shri Ashwani Kumar Prabhakar & Smt. Pratibha Prabhakar who sowed the seed of spirituality within me. My wife, Shivani, who watered those seeds and supported me in all my endeavours despite all the odds. Lastly, my children, Aryan and Aanya who have given real meaning and appropriate direction to my spiritual quest.

Contents

About the Author

Chetan Prabhakar augments happiness through conscious/mindful living (Mindfulness), and the objective of writing this book is to help people transform their lives and have true happiness by reaching a state of equanimity.

Chetan is a lawyer by profession, a monk by heart and a Modern-day Yogi. Some people also call him 'Chetan the Buddha'. He had been working as a corporate lawyer and Shivani was a homemaker and a teacher, until they finally found their true calling, 'to spread true happiness'. Chetan quit his lavish corporate career and embarked upon the journey of spreading true happiness, through the practice of Mindfulness.

It all began, when Chetan experienced the joy of mindful living, which transformed his life from being stressed, depressed, fearful, worrisome, and an angry individual to fearless, hopeful, compassionate, peaceful, and a happy individual (called "the other shore" in mindfulness practice).

Chetan Prabhakar has opened Sachetan (School of Conscious Living/Centre for Mindfulness/The Mind Gym). The primary objective of *Sachetan* is to bring true happiness in the lives of as many people as possible, through the teaching of conscious/mindful living.

Preface

We can face even the darkest period of our lives calmly, hopefully, and generate happiness even in the midst of the greatest difficulties and challenges, only if we start seeing good in the bad and bad in the good. Mind is everything and keeping mental health and hygiene is important for our minds, as a healthy mind can help us sail through every thick and thin of our life calmly and happily. Only requirement is, we need to train our mind to see the good in every situation and that is called a state of equanimity.

Nowadays, a lot of people are suffering from stress, anxiety, and depression because times have become so uncertain. Most of us might be going through rough patches of our lives with one or the other unknown and uncalled for problems. In the current circumstances, we are unaware of how to handle these situations because we have always been taught to have success and good things in our life to be happy and most of the time we do, but what if we have to face unknown circumstances and crises as we have faced during COVID 19.

Life is certainly not only about the best; it is also about the worst. Best and worst co-exist. We cannot avoid the bad and if we learn to welcome the bad as we welcome the good, we can reduce our suffering to a larger extent. Without the bad, there cannot be good, as lotus only blooms in the Mud. So, as mud is important for the lotus to blossom, similarly bad is important for the best. Imagine, if you can be happy in your worst or darkest times, how happy can you be in the good times? Just imagine!

Happiness is a mindset. We can be happy and blissful in our darkest times if we know how to keep our mind healthy in order to feed it with positivity, hopefulness and happiness. A father asks his son, do you know inside all of us there are two wolves who are always at battle with each other? The boy enquires with surprise, “Who are they?” and the father replies, “One is evil; it is anger, jealousy, greed, resentment, lies, inferiority and ego. The other is good; it is joy, peace, love, hope, kindness, empathy, compassion and truth.” The son enquires, “Which wolf wins?” The father replies, “The one you feed the most.”

We have been taught so many things but nobody has ever taught us how to keep our minds healthy and fit, which is the most important learning for everyone to have. In all the educational institutions, we have been taught everything except how to discipline the mind and keep it fit and healthy. Despite having the best of education, do we not keep on running to find true happiness throughout our lives? Do we not feel more and more miserable as we age in life? Does life not become more and more difficult as we grow up? Should our life not become better as we grow up? Should things not become easier as we age in life? That should be the outcome of our education, but, is our education not lacking this very important aspect?

We have always been taught that a healthy mind resides in a healthy body. Is this correct? I met a sports teacher who was looking quite healthy with a perfectly lean body but he said, till the time I play, I am happy and fine, but as soon as I stop playing, I have a lot of thoughts, tension and stress. So, the realization is that a healthy body may not be an abode of a healthy mind, but, a healthy mind can keep anything and everything else healthy. The actor Sushant Singh Rajput is also an example of someone who was lean and physically fit but committed suicide due to turmoil in the mind.

It does not mean that we do not have to take care of our bodies. Body is also very important and you need to take care of it as well, however, in addition, you also have to take care of your mind. You have to find the right balance. It is also important to note that it is the body's nature to deteriorate and become weak with time whereas, if taken care of, the mind grows healthy and strong.

The body and the mind are two separate entities of our being and they both need separate care, attention and exercise. As movement is good for the body similarly, stillness is good for the mind. Therefore, for holistic health, we are required to take care of both the body and the mind.

Our minds are always busy with thoughts, some belong to the future and some to the past, and hence, we are never in the present. Once a day, just try to meditate, bring your mind to the present, and try to silence the continuous chatter going on and on in the mind, which disturbs the mind and makes us confused and deluded. When our minds are silent, we can hear the quietest sound including the sound of silence and that is the real silence, and it is always internal and that silence makes us calm, composed and peaceful which are the very basis for true happiness.

If you do not keep your mind disciplined, fit and healthy, you become its servant and if you work with it, you become its master. Please note, the mind is a very good servant but a very bad master. As a master, the mind creates fears, anxiety, stress, hopelessness, unhappiness, greed, resentment, depression, etc whereas if you become its master, you can feed it with love, hope, joy, positivity, empathy, happiness, fearlessness, etc. You need to master your mind to have a wonderful life and taking care of your mind nourishes and satisfies the soul. If you do not satisfy your soul, you cannot find peace and happiness even in the midst of material and natural abundance and if your soul is satisfied, you can be your best even in the darkest days of your life.

The endeavour of this book is to help you understand that mastering the mind is important to live a life of equanimity and true happiness. To begin with, let us do a reality check as to what is a healthy mind: a healthy mind is happy; grateful; lives in the present; lets go of the past; plans the future; is positive, calm, composed and blissful; is aware, concentrated, focused and assertive.

So, these are the signs of a healthy mind. Before reading this book further, please check the condition of your mind, you may use the above parameters to understand the state of your mind at this moment and again after reading, understanding and practicing each chapter of this book; you will have to check the state of your mind using the above parameters.

Mastering the mind and reaching a stage of equanimity is the main endeavour of Monks, that is why, just be a Monk.

All the very best. May, with the end of this book, your life be transformed beyond your desires and you can smile even in the hardest days of your life.

Section A

It's all about Happiness!

One

An appointment with life

Are we fully alive? Are we really living? Most of the time, we are lost in our thoughts, in our perceptions, in the past or in the future, our body and mind working separately. Our body drives a car, but our mind thinks about something else. Physically, we are at work and mentally we are at our home and vice versa. Our body is eating but our mind is thinking. When our body and mind are not together, we are lost, we are not fully alive, we are not fully present.

Are we fully present where we are? At home, are we with children, parents and spouse, fully present, fully alive? Are we at work, fully present, both mentally and physically? Or when physically at the office, mentally, we are at home or somewhere else or when at home physically, mentally, we are at the office or somewhere else. Most of the time, we are not present in the moment and are planning or worrying for the future considering we can only take care of the future in the present.

For example, we do not see our children as they are and we are there with them with our expectations and with their future, putting a lot of pressure on them in the present for the future, so we are not fully there with them in the present as they are. Have you ever been with your children or parents with your body and mind together in the present moment? Enjoying them and being with them in the present moment, fully alive, fully aware and fully present, without any worries or tensions in the mind.

Are we really living life? Or, are we just running for the future and then when the future will come, we will again run for the future? Will this run end somewhere? Or, are we going to run this way all our lives till the time we reach our graveyards? Do we really want to meet and live life? There is an opportunity to meet life; to have an appointment with life, the same can be done by just living in the present moment. The Buddha has said, *'past is gone, future is not yet here, present is the only moment we have to live.'*

So, how can we live in the present moment? We can live in the present moment by practicing the wonderful art of right mindfulness. What does mindfulness do? It aligns our body and mind and we become fully present in the here and now. Mindfulness is simple and easy to practice. We do not have to go anywhere. We just have to come back to the present moment. Just try mindfulness by being mindful of your breath, just breathe in and out and say inside your mind while breathing in, 'I know I am breathing in', while releasing the out-breath, say, 'I know, I am breathing out', and just by doing this small exercise, body and mind get aligned. You bring your mind back to your body which is its home and when both are together, you become fully alive.

Breath is the key ingredient of mindfulness. Breath is our prana; our life force. Breath is the bridge between our mind and body. In the practice of mindfulness, we just have to be aware of our breath and it is so easy, we can inhale and exhale anywhere and everywhere and nobody will come to know what we are doing. If you have a lot of thoughts or your mind is disturbed or in tension or worry, if you breathe mindfully, your running mind stops, as breath is the halter of thoughts. So, whenever you have a lot of thoughts in your mind, worry, anxiety etc just start breathing mindfully and your thoughts will reduce manifold. It will help you calm your mind, and you will be able to get out of the mind storm and become peaceful.

The second ingredient of mindfulness is speech. When we speak in our mind, what does it do? It interrupts the continuous chattering and/or discourse which is going on and on in our mind. Hence, speaking inside our mind while breathing in and out is very important to silence our mind of unnecessary and uncalled for thoughts. We always talk about silence. The outer world can never be silent. Silence is internal. Our mind is silent when it does not have internal chatter, and because there is no chatter inside the mind, we can focus and concentrate even in the crossroads full of external noises, which will help us in becoming calm, composed and blissful.

Hence, live in the present moment and enjoy the wonders of life. Life becomes wonderful when we are fully alive. We start cherishing our children, spouse and parents because now, we are fully present with both mind and body aligned and not just with one, as most of the time, our body is present while our mind is dipped into the ocean of thoughts, perception, expectation, worry, fear etc. By being in the here and now, we can be with our loved ones and enjoy their presence because the future is uncertain and everything and everybody is impermanent, and when we start seeing impermanence and uncertainty in everything, then, there is no option to live in but to enjoy the present moment with the loved ones, that is why it is called present, which means a Gift. Living in the present moment is an appointment with life. Do not miss this appointment; for missing it is missing an opportunity for true happiness. The Buddha said:

"Nothing is more precious than being in the present moment. Fully alive, fully aware."

Practise:

Leave everything aside, straighten your spine, close your eyes and bring your awareness to your breath and while breathing in, say, 'I am breathing in', and while breathing out, say, 'I am breathing out'. Do it for a minute or more.

Note: Initially your mind will rebut as you are trying to conquer it and trying to become its master, as till now the mind is your master and no master likes to be tamed to become a servant. It will create a lot of perplexities but stick to the practise to tame and conquer it because once you conquer your mind, you will become a super soul. Verse 6.7 of the Bhagavad Gita provides as follows:

"For one who has conquered the mind, the super soul is already reached, for he has attained tranquillity. To such a man happiness and distress, heat and cold, honour and dishonour are all the same."

So, you are on a journey to become a super soul and do not stop until you really become one.

Two

Mindfulness for Happiness

Were we not born special and unique? Were we not one of the types? Were we not happy with the way we were and what we had in our childhood? But, then, slowly and steadily, we started getting conditioned to fit into the mould society has created, and, in such pursuit, we started running and left our true selves somewhere behind to become something in order to fit into the mould culture has created.

In the pursuit of becoming, most of us might be able to get desired jobs, businesses, money, power, fame, etc however, have we become truly happy after getting all that we thought would make us happy? With all the achievements and possessions comes the fear of losing them and the uncertainty of the future. Do we not sometimes get up in the middle of the night out of fear or anxiety?

You sure would agree in the affirmative. The primary reason for this occurrence is because our minds are scattered and unconquered and are behaving like drunken monkeys, who hold us back from enjoying what we have achieved and available in the here and now. Verse 6.6 of the Bhagavad Gita provides:

'For him who has conquered the mind, the mind is the best of friends; but for one who has failed to do so, his mind will remain the greatest enemy.'

So, if you wish to be truly happy, you need to conquer your mind, and how can you do that? You can conquer and tame your mind by getting into the practice of Mindfulness. The practice of Mindfulness helps us conquer our mind, which enables us to live in the present moment and experience its bliss through various easy and simple tools.

Mind is a good servant but a bad master. Through the practice of mindfulness, one can derive from the mind, what best it can do, that is to be a good servant. Neuroscience has also affirmed the benefits of mindfulness. Mindfulness perfectly aligns the body, mind and spirit, which is all it takes to be fully alive in the present moment and with a concerted focus.

Mindfulness is a profound art, yet is simple in essence. All it takes is the alignment of the mind, body and speech to reap the best from life and from yourself. It can be resorted to at any place, any time and in everything we do, such as listening, writing, eating, walking etc and our happiness is increased manifold only if we are mindful and/or aware of our breathing and the activities we perform.

And once, we have developed the habit of being mindful of our breathing and the activities we perform, we will reach a point where we will become mindful of our thoughts, feelings, emotions and perceptions and, then, once we become aware of them, we can easily convert the negative feelings, emotions, thoughts etc into positive ones, which will help us in maintaining mental hygiene, leading to increased concentration levels and focus. The results are obvious: increased productivity, elevated levels of happiness and improved quality of life.

Mindfulness is a practise to keep oneself completely present in the moment and reap its joys. There is no suffering, it is an ocean of happiness, which is endless. If we closely observe, suffering is only a by-product of living in the future or in the past. However, if we keenly notice, the present moment is a wonderful moment, where there is no suffering and most of the conditions for happiness are present.

Happiness is a habit, which has to be cultivated and nourished, and the simplest and most practical skill to cultivate and nourish happiness is MINDFULNESS.

If there is no age barrier to happiness then neither there is to this practice. It is every human's birth-right to be happy, as happiness is the prime purpose of our life since all our endeavours are in the pursuit of happiness, as such, happiness is Godliness.

Practice:

Straighten your spine, look at the tip of your nose and observe the gap between your in-breath and out-breath or the small pause between the in-breath and out-breath for 10 times or a minute.

Note: You are on a journey to become a super soul and do not stop until you really become one.

Three

Happiness is a habit

There is a friend of mine who, just after getting an excellent job, became stressed due to the high pressure in the job, fear of losing it, and uncertainty of the future if he loses the job. This stress and fear affected him so badly that it started impacting his health, personal relations, family life and sleep pattern. He started getting up at midnight in trauma with a fear of the future. Then, one day he read verse 6.7 of the Bhagavad Geeta which says:

'For one who has conquered the mind, the Super soul is already reached, for he has achieved tranquillity...'

And after reading the aforesaid verse, his search to find out the ways to conquer the mind started. And in this pursuit, he became aware of meditation as a means to control the mind. Meditation really helped him in becoming calm, composed and positive, then, he thought, why to do meditation only for one hour a day? Why not do it each and every moment, and then, he found the teaching of mindfulness which provides various simple yet effective and profound techniques as to how to meditate in each and every moment of our daily life. It is the best practise to keep oneself fully present in the here and now, where there is no suffering and many conditions of happiness are available.

You need to realise that the prime purpose of life is equanimity, and your desires to have a lot of money, power, fame, an excellent job, flourishing business, a big car, a big house etc are in the pursuit to reach a state where you are always happy and you endeavour to reach this state of eternal bliss or happiness by fulfilling your materialistic desires which will never lead you to the path of eternal bliss and happiness. Materialism and Spiritualism are two wings and without either, you will not be able to take the flight for reaching a state of equanimity where lies the true happiness and eternal bliss.

In this endeavour of achieving happiness through materialism, we all think or have been conditioned to think that we will be happy only after fulfilment of our materialist desires, but has our search for happiness stopped or have we become truly happy? The answer probably is "No" because we are always postponing happiness for something or the other. On the other hand, even after getting all the things desired, we become more tensed, stressed, caught up, trapped etc as now there arises a fear of either losing them, not being able to maintain them, or not growing any further, or what people will say if we do not have this or that, so the real struggle of life starts.

This is actually not life; life is different; life is beautiful, life is happiness, pure bliss, but how can we be always happy/blissful? It is not possible to be happy in each and every moment. Isn't it? How can we be happy without having all material comforts or without growing in our career or having a big car/house or a lot of money, power or fame? The answer is, we all have desires for financial, social and material well-being and, we all need money, status and material things to have a good life, the only difference we need to make is not to become a slave to these things, get attached and keep running. If we become mindful, we will start appreciating and enjoying each and every moment of life, and will enjoy what we have achieved till now.

Once we are mindful in each and every moment, we become the master of our minds and once we have become the masters of our minds, is everything not possible? The answer probably is "Yes". If we are mindful, and fully present in the here and now, and become aware of our thoughts and perceptions, we will be more productive because we have no extra thinking such as regret of the past or fear of the future, as now we know how to take care of negative feelings, emotions and thinking and convert the same to positive ones, which will result in fewer distractions, increased focus and concentration on the work in hand.

We will probably do much more work in lesser time than earlier. Will this not lead to success, growth, abundance and what not? And in addition, we can enjoy what we have to the fullest and always be happy. Happiness is a state of mind and a choice. Like all other habits, happiness is also a habit. Remaining tense and unhappy is easy and it is the habit of a lazy mind, and a mind which is alert and aware can always choose to be happy. As Venerable Zen Master, Thich Nhat Hanh says,

"Happiness is available. Please help yourself to it."

Practice:

Smile in awareness. Smile because it is a mouth yoga and relaxes hundreds of muscles on your face, so smile, Buddha has said, "*sometimes joy is the source of your smile and sometimes smile is the source of your joy." Enjoy!*

Four

Awareness-A key to Happiness

Awareness is one of the key ingredients of Dhyana Yoga in Hinduism, Zen in Buddhism, Sufism in Islam and Surati in Sikhism. Hindus call it Sakshin (witnessing), Buddhists call it Samyak Samriti (right mindfulness), Saint Kabir and Guru Nanak call it Surati (remembrance), and Sufis call it Jikr (remembrance), but they all talk about Awareness. The similarities between these philosophies are that we have to be aware and keep observing our thoughts, perceptions and feelings to wake ourselves spiritually and live in eternal bliss.

As I am promoting true happiness through the practise of Mindfulness, here, I will elaborate on Samyak Samriti (right mindfulness) which is a practise of Zen Buddhism. As you must have become aware by now, the practise of Mindfulness offers various simple, easy, logical and practical tools to enlighten ourselves, attain true happiness and live-in eternal bliss. Mindfulness is so easy as it can become part of your daily routine without any extra effort. As a first step, you only need to be mindful and/or aware of your breath, which is the most important thing. When we are born, we take our first breath and when we die, we take our last breath in awareness, and in between, we just forget to acknowledge or be aware of our breath. Breath is a bridge between our body and mind. It aligns our body and mind, and as said earlier, when our body and mind are aligned, we become fully aware and alive.

Once we become aware of our breath, then, slowly and steadily, we can become mindful of our day-to-day activities such as eating, drinking, walking, sitting etc. Once somebody asked Buddha, what do you and your monks do? We breathe, walk, talk, eat, drink etc, the Buddha replied. The man enquired, what is so special in that? Everybody else is doing so. The only difference is, we do these things in awareness. The Buddha replied.

While practicing mindfulness, we can start our day just by observing our breath; watching the sky, sun, birds, plants, flowers etc; hearing the chirping of birds, sound of air, voices near and far to wake all our senses. By being mindful of nature, which is called the Kingdom of God in mindfulness practice, we can automatically become mindful of our inner world. The keyword is 'awareness' of our inner world by observing the nature outside, which is also helpful in developing a habit to observe activities of our body and mind.

Once we become aware of our breath and day-to-day activities, our mind develops a habit of awareness and then, it will automatically start observing thoughts, perceptions and feelings and then, we can easily convert our negative feelings and thoughts into positive ones and suffering into true happiness. The four noble truths are 1) suffering exists; 2) there are reasons for suffering; 3) happiness also exists and; 4) there is a path leading to happiness. And right mindfulness is such a path that leads to true happiness.

Practice:

Bring awareness to your thoughts and make a list of your thoughts by labelling them as positive and negative and a list of thoughts that make you suffer.

Five

You are Unique!

Why are we here on the earth? We are here to fulfil a special purpose of the creator and to reach a state of eternal happiness, bliss and equanimity. This state is achieved merely by finding our true self, nature and uniqueness.

We go through stress, pressure and tension throughout our lives. We slough day in and out to become something in order to show people whom either we do not like or who do not like us, because for the people who love us they love us the way we are.

This is what life has become, and in the end, we realize that our life has gone charming others, doing things we never wanted to do and alas, we could have the courage to change it earlier. We all must have seen many old people who despite having shouldered all their responsibilities are still worried, tense, have regrets, etc. This is what we do in our life, we keep on regretting the past and worrying about the future and when the future comes, then also, we keep on worrying about the future and it becomes a never-ending process.

We need to ponder on a question. Is life meant for all this? Is life not meant to be unique as the way the Universe has created us? Is there anybody in the world exactly like you? Just try to find even one person who is exactly like you in all aspects. It is guaranteed that you will not find one, then, why do we think that the same education, same occupation and same conditioning will help us in growing well and becoming truly happy.

With your uniqueness comes your unique talent and purpose for which the universe has created you and sent you in this world and only if you find your true nature, uniqueness, unique talent and that special purpose for which you were created, you will reach a state where there is eternal bliss and happiness.

As a reminder again, are we not trying to find happiness throughout our lives, but, somehow due to cultural conditioning, are we not losing ourselves? Are we not feeling more and more miserable as we are ageing? Is life not becoming more and more difficult as we are growing up? Should our life not become better as we grow up? Should things not become easier as we age in life? Should our kids not look at us and really want to grow up as happy human beings like us? If the answer is yes, then, how can we achieve all this?

Have your old thinking patterns, habits, concepts, perceptions and beliefs helped you so far to become truly happy and blissful? Perhaps not, and if not, then, first of all, you should endeavour to change your conditioned thinking, views, perceptions, concepts etc and this will happen only by changing the patterns stored in your mind.

The practise of mindfulness helps you to change the old rotten patterns of your mind which stop you from being happy in each and every moment. The practise of Mindfulness can help you transform your life by knowing your true self, uniqueness and your higher purpose and as a result, you will become truly happy and blissful.

Practice:

From now onwards for about a week, try to find a single person who is exactly like you. If you don't find one, increase your quest to find your true self, your unique talent and the higher purpose for which the Universe has created you.

Section B

Mind is everything!

Six

Tame the Monkey Mind!

Stress, anxiety and depression have become the most common words nowadays because a lot of people are suffering from these conditions. An example of extreme depression was the case of an actor, who was found hanging himself in his apartment in Mumbai. Two important questions arise from this unfortunate incident; 1) why people suffer from stress, anxiety and depression and why do people having success, fame, money and power suffer from these illnesses when these things are considered as a sure sign of success, security and happiness? We have to look at the root causes of this disturbing problem.

To start with, let us understand what is stress, anxiety and depression. Stress, anxiety and depression together become 'SAD'. In layman's language, stress means a state of a mental condition resulting from adverse or demanding circumstances. Increase in stress can cause anxiety and depression. Anxiety means repetition of negative or fearful thoughts because of a particular event or its outcome and an increase in anxiety can cause depression. Depression means having a lot of thoughts and most of them being negative. It means a continuous negative chatter going on and on in the mind, which becomes an uncontrollable process, and the person keeps getting deeper into the ocean of negativity and does not know how to get out of it. Thoughts become deep, continuous and never-ending. There is loss of confidence, increase in sadness, lower self-esteem, lower motivation and enthusiasm levels. Life becomes an ocean of suffering and sometimes, thoughts become suicidal and in extreme circumstances, the person commits suicide.

One of the root causes of all this can be our education and cultural conditioning which is busy preparing and motivating us towards success, fame, money, power etc considering that only success, money, power, fame etc shall make us happy. But, is this true? Have these materialistic things made us truly happy? The probable answer is 'no' because happiness doesn't entirely depend upon materialism or external circumstances.

We can be happy in whatever circumstances or conditions we are in because happiness is a habit which we need to cultivate and nourish. Happiness also doesn't depend upon success or failure in jobs, businesses, relationships etc and is purely a state of mind. We should learn to accept and embrace our failures as we embrace our success, because success and failure are two sides of a coin, as such, they co-exist and are a part and parcel of our lives. Our education should also teach us to celebrate our failures as well as provide us with a perspective that it is okay to fail and there is no benefit in feeling remorse for it. What can go wrong will go wrong.

Why worry because there is always light after darkness. Challenges come to make us strong, so, when there are challenges in your life, try to be strong and face the challenge boldly. Every storm passes by and time never remains the same.

We have also been conditioned to postpone our happiness from one thing to another, and we keep on delaying our happiness to the future accomplishments, thinking that if I will get this degree; if I will get that car; if I will get the promotion; if I will get a bigger house and et al, then, I will be happy and in such a way, we keep on postponing our happiness to the future and never get it because we make our happiness dependent on our achievements and even after accomplishing what we wanted we again have new desires for which we again postpone our happiness to their fulfilment and in a way, running for happiness becomes our habit. When we do not know how to be happy without depending on fulfilment of our desires and materialistic things, success, fame, money etc and we keep worrying about them and the future, we easily fall prey to these mental ailments.

We need to understand that stress, anxiety and depression are illnesses of the mind. And are we taking enough care of our minds? Are we giving enough time to our minds? Can physical exercises alone help us in curing these mental illnesses? Through physical exercises, the body becomes active and the mind becomes active and restless, however, the right balance should be an active body and calm mind, because an active or restless mind creates many thoughts which are not good for our mental health and hygiene. As movement is good for the body; similarly, stillness is good for the mind. Therefore, the mind needs separate exercises and workouts. The more you still your body, the more your mind relaxes and becomes calm and peaceful.

Does medical science provide any help in curing stress, anxiety and depression? To a certain extent, it may be. Medical science mostly deals with the ailment of the human body; however, thoughts, feelings, emotions, concepts and perceptions are part of mind/consciousness, and for these, there can be no medicine that can deal with and transform our negative thoughts, feelings, emotions into positive ones. Hence treating stress, anxiety and depression only with medicines is like launching an arrow in the sky that will hit nowhere. Medicines can only put you to sleep for some time and slowly and gradually, you become addicted and dependent upon these medicines, however, the depression remains uncured. Medicine can only be used as an aid in curing these mental illnesses but without exercises of mind, these conditions cannot be completely cured.

The only way to cure stress, anxiety and depression is through self-help by way of doing some exercises for the mind, and one of such self-help practices is Mindfulness. Mindfulness or Dhyana yoga can help in managing or curing these illnesses without any addictive medicines and/or drugs.

To come out of the aforesaid conditions, we need to practice Mindfulness. Mindfulness helps us in reducing thoughts. Mindfulness works in the same manner as an air-conditioner works. It does not fight with the heat but slowly and gradually increases the cool air which results in rid from the heat. In a similar way, as the mindfulness will increase, the continuous negative babble going on and on inside our minds will decrease resulting in a healthy mind.

To have a healthy mind, you have to tame your mind which behaves like a drunken monkey. The only way to tame the monkey mind is living in the present moment, and once you have tamed it, you will become the master of your mind, and once you have mastered your mind, then a) you are always aware of your negative thoughts, perceptions and feelings; b) you know a way to convert them into positive ones; c) this helps in increasing positivity, confidence and self-esteem and; d) the ultimate result is eternal happiness and bliss.

Practice:

Check your tongue and if it is stuck to the upper part of your mouth, remove it from there, keep it in the middle and be aware.

Light an incense stick and become aware of its fragrance and listen to soothing music and feel it within you.

Seven

Selecting the seeds, we water

We all have good and bad seeds in our mind, such as seeds of love, beauty, grace, happiness, hopefulness, etc and also seeds of anger, ego, greed, fear, worry, etc. And the seeds we water more will grow, such as, if we water the seed of hate, hate will grow, and, if we water the seed of love, love will grow. An old proverb provides as follows:

"*There is a battle of two wolves inside all of us. One is evil. It is anger, jealousy, greed, resentment, lies, inferiority, and ego. The other is good. It is joy, peace, love, hope, kindness, empathy and truth.*

The wolf that wins? The one you feed."

So, we need to be very conscious and mindful in selecting the seeds we water. Every human being is born with all types of seeds, and it depends upon the grooming and/or the environment in which such a person grows as the mind picks up and consumes different seeds from the environment, we are in.

Now, let us evaluate how can we have selective watering of seeds? By following simple steps of mindfulness, we can have selective watering. It is very important to know what selective watering is, and the same can be explained in the following manner:

We have consciousness and the same has two parts; one is store or subconsciousness and; the other is mind consciousness. In the store/subconsciousness, we have all the seeds such as anger, ego, resentment, love, hopefulness, beauty, happiness, etc. Now, the store consciousness throws seeds to the conscious mind based on our consumption from different modes or senses, such as, if we have consumed from the environment fear, worry, anger, etc it will throw these seeds to the conscious minds, which the conscious mind will pick up and then by constant thinking multiply it manifold.

Buddha explained this in the following manner:

Suppose a man is hit by an arrow, now instead of taking this arrow out, he is being hit by many other arrows, so what will happen? Obviously, his pain and suffering will multiply, and if the arrow is removed, the pain will reduce and he will feel relieved, similarly, when our conscious mind gets hit by seeds of fear, anger, despair etc and if we keep on watering these seeds, they will grow and become trees. For e.g let's talk about a circumstance, despite doing everything for your family, friends or colleagues at home or in the office you are never appreciated and always criticized. Now, you have a seed of suffering. Let us understand here, how it will be watered? You start talking about your suffering with your other friends, relatives, colleagues etc and some of them may have similar experiences or sufferings too and they will also share their pain and/or suffering. You watch a TV programme or listen to the radio or read the news which has similar incidents or events and the same resonate with your pain and suffering. This is how you water these seeds and they will grow manifold, then, it will create frustration, worry, stress, anxiety and pain, and under such distress, you may take many steps in haste and/or anger, which will create more afflictions, despair and sufferings.

On the other hand, if you know the art of mindfulness, you will take the arrow out, apply an ointment, get some rest and now, the suffering is gone. In a similar way, in the above-mentioned condition, if you know this art, you will become aware that you have seeds of frustration, worry or pain at the level of your mind consciousness and then, by using the tools of mindfulness, you will replace it with good and wholesome seeds by going out to some good place; listening to some good music; reading something positive; meditating, sitting, lying or walking; appreciating good things and recognizing conditions of happiness already present in your life, and in this way, you will heal the suffering. And by doing so, you will water the positive seeds which have converted your suffering into happiness. Venerable Eminent Zen Master Thich Nhat Hanh, Father of Mindfulness says as follows:

'Because suffering is impermanent, that is why we can transform it. because happiness is impermanent, that is why we have to nourish it.

Practice:

Change your consumption. If you watch television. Change the channels you watch. Switch to a travel channel or cookery show and after some time you will find yourself either cooking or travelling.

Eight

Future is uncertain, get surprised

We all have a fear of the future as the future is uncertain, and as conditioned human beings, we prefer familiar suffering to uncertainties. There is a story of a man who used to pray to God to reach the peak of a mountain, and one day, God acceded his prayers, picked him up and left him on the peak, now, at night while walking this man lost his balance. While falling down, he got hold of a tree, thinking that there was an abyss in which he would fall. He again prayed to God for help. God came and said, "Leave this tree," but now, this man did not even believe in God, and said, "How can I leave this? If I leave, I will fall down and die." God acceded to his wish and left. Now, when the sun rose in the morning, in the sunlight, the man saw that there was a good small plateau just a few inches below his feet, where he could have rested the entire night.

We all are like this man, we believe in God for everything, but don't believe him when it is about the future, its fears and uncertainties. We want to make sure that we take care of the future in the present and do not actually live the present. We try to teach our kids that study today to have a bright future, and give them a lot of stress in the present. We work too much and remain in stress in the present and save money for the future because we have been conditioned to think that the future will only bring rainy days, and then when the future comes, we again run for the future and running becomes a never-ending process and we realize this when we reach the end of our lives. Can we stop running and really live our life which is available in the present moment.

Future doesn't always bring rainy days. I am not saying that we should not plan for the future but we should not worry about the future and give more importance to the future than the present. Mind is everything, what we think we become. If we think the future will bring rainy days, it is definitely going to bring rainy days and if we think, the future is going to be beautiful, it is going to be beautiful. Just live the present moment to the fullest which in itself is a preparation for the future. Enjoy your present to enjoy your future. Nobody knows what happens in the future. Nobody knows if we will be there for the future because everything is impermanent so as we and our loved ones are. So, if we don't spend a good time with them in the present, what is the assurance that we will ever have lovely moments in the future? Memories can only be made in the present moment. The present moment is the only moment which we can live as per our wish as the future is usually uncertain. It is better to be surprised by the future than to predict it. Because a predictable future cannot bring anything surprising and interesting.

We all are concerned and busy making money but has money actually brought true happiness in our lives? Success without happiness is nothing. If we become successful and not happy, does success make any meaning in life and on the other hand, if we become truly happy then we can also enjoy our success. So, let us try to become happy before being successful in order for us to enjoy our success. Let us meditate and use spirituality to become truly happy. The venerable Sir Sri Paramhansa Yogananda has given two approaches for life:

'Money first; God can come later! Who knows? Life may be too long.

God first, money is his slave! Who can tell? Life may be too short.'

Hence, we need to be mindful to adopt one of the aforesaid approaches in life. We are running after success as we think being successful shall make us happy but it is otherwise. True happiness will bring real success in our lives. As Happiness is the prime purpose of human life, hence, Happiness is Godliness. And Mindfulness is one of the easiest paths which can lead us to true happiness. Mindfulness is an art that will help you work on your karma in the present. Karma is not only physical action, but Karma is of three kinds which are thought karma, speech karma and action karma. Thought is the beginning of karma so if we work on our thoughts and keep them positive, our speech and action karma will become positive. Hence, the practise of mindfulness will keep you positive in every situation and will give you the ability and confidence to change the things which you cannot accept and accept the things which you cannot change which will give you wings to fly and live a happy and successful life. As it is said, 'be happy now, success will follow, do not fear the future, as the future is uncertain, be surprised by it.

Practise:

Just rewind your life and see how your life continued and try to find out how much did you plan and did everything happen as per your planning? Just reflect.

Section C

Let us feed the Good Wolf

Nine

Concentration, develop it

A lot of people say that they lack concentration and this is because they have some kind of disorder. I have heard many doctors saying this to their patients and these patients do start believing and living in such a mindset that they have a disorder. Is that true? Is lack of concentration some kind of disorder?

To answer this, we need to understand what concentration really means. Does concentration mean doing things with full focus? Does concentration mean to concentrate our mind on whatever we are doing? Concertation means if we are reading, we are just reading. Concentration means focus and one-pointedness. Concentration means developing awareness of our activities.

If we are reading and thinking about something else, we are not concentrating. If we are eating and thinking about something else, we are not concentrating. If we are walking and have other things in mind, we are not concentrating. In view of these, if we go by doctors, all the human race lacks concentration and has a disorder.

The good news is, lack of concentration is not a disorder. It is just that we have not trained our minds to be concentrated as societal conditioning has promoted the concept of multitasking as some kind of intelligence. Because of this, we have been multitasking in everything: we are driving a car and speaking on the phone; eating our food and watching TV or talking; walking on the road but thinking about something else and et al. In reality, nobody lacks concentration, on the other hand, the most appropriate way to say is that nobody develops concentration. Concentration, focus and one-pointedness are developed. Some may have this inherent talent but others have to develop this.

Also, what is one of the most common reasons for a lack of concentration? It is that most of the time, we are also compelled to do thing/s which we don't like. We all are different with unique personalities, interests and temperaments, however, due to peer pressure, societal conditioning and demand of old patterns and culture, most of us including kids are compelled to do things that we do not like, that is why we lack concentration as we lack interest in what we are doing. Once try to do a thing which you really love and see how much you can concentrate.

However, now as many of us have really grown up, and may also have started living with the belief that we lack concentration. So, now, if we wish to have the power of concentration which will improve the quality of our life we need to know how to develop and increase our concentration power. There is a concept called Moment to Moment Concertation (MTMC), which means in every moment we are concentrated. Whatever we are doing, we are concentrated and that is the best way to develop concentration, and the best practice to develop moment-to-moment concentration is Mindfulness.

The practice of mindfulness can help us develop concentration. We have to start by being mindful or aware of every activity we are performing. In mindfulness, we believe that we can meditate everywhere and in anything and everything. In this practice, for everything and anything, we have meditation. The literal meaning of meditation is Dhyana which means to be concentrated and aware, however, if we have to meditate, we have to have the power of concentration that is why in this practice, we say that every activity is an opportunity for meditation if we do it in awareness. Awareness and concertation go hand in hand. If we become aware of our activities, we will automatically become concentrated. Awareness increases concentration and concentration increases awareness; therefore, both complement each other.

We all think that when we sit cross-legged and concentrate or focus on something that is mediation, but, in mindfulness practice, we say that if we concentrate on anything it becomes meditation. In mindfulness practice, everything is meditation and every day-to-day activity is an opportunity for meditation, such as, while walking we can do walking meditation, while eating we can do eating meditation, while calling someone we can do calling meditation, when drinking tea, water or anything else of our choice we can do drinking meditation and while sleeping we can do total relaxation meditation.

The keyword to develop concentration is one task at a time. Just start doing one thing at a moment, and you will see how focused and concentrated you become. To start with, while eating your food, just see your food for a few seconds, see the texture of the food and then start eating your food slowly and in full awareness. Have the real taste of the food and then see how concentrated you become. When attending a phone call, just take three in and out breaths and then, pick up the phone and as a piece of caution do not drive when talking on the phone. It is important to know that when we are concentrated, focused and mindful while driving we can avoid accidents. The only reason for accidents is that our body drives a car but our mind is somewhere else; in the past, future, home or office.

Lack of concentration is not a disorder as concentration needs to be developed. We have never been taught how to concentrate. No school is teaching concentration, focus and one-pointedness, then, how will we learn concentration. Schools should add concentration practice in the curriculum. You should also stop complaining that you or your kids lack concentration. On the other hand, you should start developing concentration power which shall improve the quality of your life manifold. You will become more productive as with the development of concentration, you will have fewer distractions in the mind.

The practice of right mindfulness helps us to concentrate and when we are concentrated, our mind becomes silent which means the internal chatter or discourse going on and on in our mind stops. And when our mind is silent, we achieve real peace of mind. External world can never be silent, silence is internal and when we develop the power of mindfulness, then we can focus and concentrate even on busy roads full of external noises. This is what mindfulness does; it increases focus, concentration and one-pointedness which in turn silent the chatter going on inside our minds. When our mind becomes silent, there are less distractions, and with less distraction, you will be able to learn more and understand things faster and also meet the challenges of life with ease. Swami Vivekanand has said, *'the power of concentration, is the only key to the treasure-house of knowledge. Through concentration of mind everything can be accomplished even mountains can be crushed to atoms.'*

Practice:

Look at a point or object or a light bulb or candlelight for a few seconds without blinking your eyes, then close your eyes and try to see the Object/Light in between your eyebrows.

Ten

Non-discrimination, adopt it

Should we do this or should we do that, is a question we are often faced with. And in the desire to take upon the right path, we burden our mind with contingencies, what if this, what if that, and confusion sets in and we find ourselves sinking in the swamp rather than getting out of it.

This or that, good or bad, right or left, right or wrong, pure or impure, all these are the two sides of a coin. Without left, there cannot be right, neither can good exist without bad, likewise, without poor the rich cannot exist and without impure there can be no pure. Everything has its own importance. They co-exist, that is why, mother earth never discriminates between them. We cannot only have good, for with good co-exists bad. We either embrace both or we get none. God has created something for everybody. Therefore, there always are two sides to everything, something bad for one can be good for another, such as, rain is bad for a person who has a plan for a picnic, but, at the same time that rain is good for the farmer whose field is parched.

Similarly, if there is only good, good will lose its identity. In fact, the Universe has created everything as per the need of human beings, however, human beings have made good-bad, right-wrong, pure-impure etc as per their needs, likings, desires, concepts and perceptions. Lot of people ask me if we can be spiritual and have non-vegetarian food. I always find it difficult to answer, but, the real answer can be a question; how will people survive in a place where there is no vegetation and eating non-vegetarian food is not a choice but a compulsion? So, for them, this is a matter of survival and if they have to eat this food in compulsion, then, in such a case, can they not be spiritual? Spirituality is about getting connected to our soul and everyone has one, so everyone can be spiritual. Caste, creed, race, religion, food habits or other habits are no restraints for spirituality. Consume whatever you want to, do whatever you want to, so long it makes your soul happy. Plants are also living beings, they too breathe, they have a life, then, how can killing a plant be good? Just because their pain can't be heard or their suffering seen, it does not mean that they feel no pain, they have no agony.

On the path of spirituality, the only thing we need to be cautious about is distinguishing between good and bad, right and wrong, pure and impure etc. As the moment we fall into the trap of marking such distinctions, we start creating delusions in our minds which are the first hindrances on the path of awakening. Just accept everything as it is, including yourself, to make steadfast progress on the way of awakening.

A great awakening is awaiting you. The only requirement is a conscious effort to conquer your minds through meditation and mindful/conscious living to awaken yourself spiritually to have eternal bliss and tranquillity.

Practice:

Ask yourself a question: What if I could have been born to a different parent or in a different country? Suppose, you were born in India or the US, ask yourself a question, what if I was born in New Zealand or London or Pakistan? Would I be the same person who I am now and would I have the same belief system as I have now?

Eleven

Gratitude work wonders, practice it

We all have more than sufficient conditions to be grateful, however, most of the time we find ourselves complaining about the things missing in our life. If we keenly observe, 80% of the things in our life are perfectly fine, however, instead of being grateful to the Universe for the things we have, we complain about the 20% of things we may not have.

Let us assume that despite doing everything you can do for your family, friends and relatives, what you always listen to is complaints, what will happen to you. In the similar way, despite getting more than what is needed, we always complain about the things we do not have. What may be the feelings of the Creator?

Gratitude or being grateful is a habit, which we need to develop for receiving more in life. When we become grateful for what the Universe has given us, it feels appreciated and becomes happy, and starts giving us more. Gratitude is a practice that also helps us to grow in life by leaps and bounds.

Start your days by saying to God that I am grateful for getting up this morning, and say thanks to God for the food you and shelter you have. Many people do not have that. Being grateful is key for an abundant and happy life. If you wish to have prosperity, abundance and happiness in life, be grateful for what you have now and enjoy; keep saying thanks to God for everything you have and even for the undesirable things that happen in your life because misfortune will bring fortune and visa-versa.

Whenever you feel sad or low or feel like life is not good, start writing and make a list of all the good things you have in life, and you will notice that your mood will improve and you will become happy and elated. And, if you start making a list of gratitude as a regular practice, you will see that the list of things for which you are grateful is increasing day by day.

Please keep in your mind, God also needs appreciation as we all need. So, keep saying thanks to God for everything and see the difference in your life, your life will become a wonder and you will be jubilant. That is the wonder of gratitude. Be grateful to God and be prosperous, abundant and happy.

Practice:

Write down a list of things you can be grateful for, example can be your body, your eyes which can see well, your kids, your paycheque, a roof over your head, a car or bike to drive etc. Think about a person who does not have what all you have.

Twelve

Letting go is easy

We stick to things; to material possessions; to our views, concepts and perceptions and most of the time, we keep sticking to them irrespective of the fact that they may be creating suffering for us. We choose to suffer than to release them and let them go.

Once the Buddha was sitting with his monks in the forest when a farmer passed by in a great hurry and was very much worried. He asked the Buddha and monks if they have seen his cows passing by, as in the morning; all of his cows ran away and he does not know their whereabouts and is very worried as those cows were the only source of livelihood for him. The Buddha replied with great compassion that he has not seen the cows and the farmer can see them in the other direction, and then, the Buddha turned to his monks and said, "you are very lucky, you do not have cows." Here, the Buddha refers to cows as attachments.

The Buddha teaches that our attachments are our cows and we need to release them and let them go if they make us suffer. Things that make us suffer and do not give us true happiness are our cows and we need to recognize them and let them go. Everything which is not giving us happiness, we need to release them because sticking to them creates attachments and attachments are the root cause of our suffering. Let go of your attachments and you will be happy. Do not depend upon your attachments for happiness.

The biggest cause of attachment is our views, concepts and perception and we are not ready to release them despite the fact that they are making us suffer. The reason we keep on suffering than letting them go is because we don't know how to do it. We don't know how to release these cows and be happy. We have been conditioned that way and our society is also conditioned in such a way, which also does not let us release our attachments because doing so will not jell with the cultural conditioning.

We are also fearful of uncertainties that is why we prefer familiar suffering to uncertainties. Yes, uncertainty creates fears but if we really open up to uncertainties, it will give us surprises. Miracles can only happen in uncertainty. Predictability cannot give surprises and miracles. Embrace uncertainty, let go of attachment and predictable future. Happiness comes when we let go and release all our attachments and fears and embrace uncertainty.

We need to practice letting go and the practice to let go is to live in the moment and let go of the fear of the future and its uncertainty. Let go of everything which is the outcome of your psychological fears and fear of uncertainties to have a wonderful and blissful life.

Practice:

Make a list of materialistic things which you are afraid to lose and then among those things, try to give away one thing which you can easily give up. Give it to someone needy and/or unknown to you.

Thirteen

Transcend False Ego for Bliss

False Ego is a self-image or false image which we have created for ourselves out of our conditioning, education, material possessions, success, grooming, ranks etc and conditioning of this ego starts from the time we are born. Recall yourself as a three to four years old baby. Did you have the same personality or thinking as you have now? Were you not more loving and compassionate without bothering as to what people would think?

We also drive false ego from the materialistic things we have or the position we carry in the society such as I am a Doctor, Lawyer, Saint, Officer, Minister etc and we hide our true self behind this false and temporary image. We also drive false ego in getting respect from others such as I am the father or elder brother or a senior so I deserve respect and people should listen to me. This is also false ego.

We also develop false ego by trying to fit into the mould society has created, even if it does not give us satisfaction or liberation in the true sense. Despite the suffering, we do not change ourselves. Sticking to our own views, concepts and perceptions, even if they are not solving any purpose is also ego. Buddha has said, '*we prefer familiar suffering, than to face uncertainties, because, we have attachments and these attachments create fear of uncertainty or becoming nothing or losing everything we have and desiring things to be permanent or being always right and good is also false ego.*'

We need to transcend this false ego to have a blissful life and the first step is to reduce attachments including tangible and intangible. Verse 2.71 of the Bhagavad Gita stipulates, '*a person who has given up all desires for sense gratification, who lives free from desires, who has given up all sense of proprietorship and is devoid of false ego – he alone can attain real peace.*'

When we transcend ego, we go beyond our fears of what people will think, and that is important for spiritual awakening because we can only transcend ego once we become our true selves and we accept everything as it is including ourselves. We become a person of no rank. We do not recognize ourselves with ranks, material possession, status or education and then, we go from impression to expression, competition to creation, confusion to confidence and delusion to clarity that is what, transcending ego means.

To transcend false ego, we need to reduce our attachments as our attachments are the major cause of our suffering and the tool to reduce attachment is 'Giving' and the best way to transcend false ego is to give away the things which we fear losing the most. Once the Buddha was sitting with his monks in the forest when a farmer passed by in a great hurry and was very much worried. He asked the Buddha and monks if they have seen his cows passing by, as in the morning; all of his cows ran away and he does not know their whereabouts and is very worried as those cows were the only source of livelihood for him. The Buddha replied with great compassion, that he has not seen the cows and the farmer can see them in the other direction, and then, the Buddha turned to his monks and said, 'you are very lucky, you do not have cows.' Here, the Buddha refers to cows as attachments.

Giving is also important to awaken ourselves spiritually. As giving reduces false ego and transcending false ego always remains the last step to awaken ourselves spiritually. And once false ego is transcended, a person becomes the Buddha.

Let us give. Let us give even when we don't have enough. Giving increases the validation of our good Karma. The universe knows only one law that is the law of give and take which is also the law of cause and effect. What we give, we get back in one form or the other. Giving is a practice that reduces our attachments. Whatever you can give, just give and give without expectation. Give anything and everything; give a compliment, a smile, something material but give. Giving itself is important, so, just give. It is said, takers may eat well but givers sleep well. So, give, give and give.

Give secretly. Give in a manner that nobody comes to know who has given. Give in a manner where the taker has no clue of receiving, because, if we give to show that we are giving then that is running after an image which will increase our ego and not reduce it and transcending ego is a way to spiritual enlightenment and eternal bliss, because, when we are spiritually enlightened, we are always in bliss and that bliss is divine and that happiness and bliss is without any rhyme or reason. That is the state where we all need to reach before we die. We need to be in eternal bliss.

Practise

Give secretly, take a currency note of whatever denomination you can afford, roll it, put a slip in it saying, 'this is your happy money' and keep it somewhere secretly where somebody can find it. Do not try to see who finds it. After keeping it, immediately move from there. If you cannot afford to give money, you can keep some food or clothes.

Section D

Parenting is an Art!

Fourteen

Mindful Parenting

Do you hug your kids every day? Like breakfast, lunch and dinner, hugs should be made part of the daily routine. The mindful way to hug is to breathe thrice while you hug your child. It is a kind of a reminder that conveys in a non-verbal way to the child, darling, I am here for you.

Do you spend quality time with your kids? Quality time is a time which we spend with our kids when they need us. We have to be with them when they need us emotionally, mentally and physically. We often ignore the demand of our kids when they need us, such as, they want us to play or talk and as we have other occupations, we often ignore their demands and divert their attention to what we expect from them. As parents, it is more important to understand the needs of our children than forcing them to do what we expect and think is right.

Most of the time, when we reach home our bodies are there but our minds are somewhere else. We meet our children with our expectations, worries about the future and their career. As parents, we often forget that our children have a present too and in the worry of taking care of their future, we are not heeding to their present and we miss them in the present as they are. That's why it is often said that children grow up very fast. This is because we focus a lot on the future and never enjoy their present. Hence, a hug when you or your child reach home is a recognition of appreciating their present.

We often have expectations for our kids to perform well academically and otherwise also, for them to have a bright future, and we, as parents, often do so in pressure of our society, friends and relatives; and of course, with a fear that our kids should not lag behind and what people will think. In such a pursuit, we want our kids to run a race and win it which they may inherently not be meant for. Have we ever observed our kids as they are, what are their inherent interests and unique talents? Jiddu Krishnamurti has said, *'Nature is busy creating absolutely unique individuals, whereas culture has invented a single mould to which all must conform. It is grotesque.'*

Every child is unique with a different purpose in life. They have their only intelligence and their intelligence is pure; not influenced and conditioned. I would like to share an incident with you. Once in my office, we had a debate as to who is a true leader. There were different views, such as, a leader should be an influencer; a true leader produces a leader; a true leader has followers etc and the same day, I had the fortune to learn the pure and real definition of a leader from my five-year-old son who was made monitor of his class. When I reached home from work, he said, "Mama, today I have been appointed as a monitor of my class." I applauded in happiness and pride. Suddenly, my son said, "But I don't want to be a monitor because a monitor has to work for everyone." Isn't this a real definition of a leader as a leader has to work for everyone? After this incident, I have now started learning from my son and younger daughter too. Whenever I have a difficult situation and/or I am confused, I go to my kids and ask them for solutions, and you know, I always get some great and unique ideas.

We also need to understand that education should be a means to life skills which are confidence, positivity, to know oneself and to know how to live and celebrate life. Some children perform academically or otherwise well in the early stages of their life and some perform well in the later stages of their life, and therefore, there should be no comparison. We should be patient and should not put any pressure on the child to win the race which is not in his/her inherent nature and they should be given enough space and time to create their own unique personality.

Now is the time when we should stop conditioning our children with rotten education, old culture and societal conditioning. Let them grow as they are and be their true selves, and if they are their true selves, they will really grow as unique individuals with extraordinary success and happiness. Our only job as parents is to observe, support and guide them in whatever they want to do and not what we think they should do; however, the most important thing is, you should gift them your presence; a real presence by giving them a mindful hug every day by saying inside your mind, 'Darling, I am here for you.'

Practise:

Give a hug to your child and while giving the hug, breathe in and out thrice and say inside your mind, 'Darling, I am here for you.'

Fifteen

Modern-day Parenting

Every kid is unique and a genius with different abilities and talents and only academic excellence should not be made a measure of intelligence and/or success. As Albert Einstein has said, *'Everyone is genius. But if you judge a fish by its ability to climb a tree, it will live its whole life believing that it is stupid.'*

Parenting is an art and it is not about raising children, it is about raising parents. As time has changed, we also need to change conventional parenting to modern-day parenting. Few tips for modern-day parenting are as follows:

Let's treat our children respectfully like individuals and also respect their individuality and uniqueness. This will help them to grow as individuals with self-respect and esteem.

We should at no cost scare them or make them fearful about anything including their results in examinations and/or their future because fear kills creativity in children which in turn makes them underconfident and have low self-esteem.

To nurture creativity and holistic development other than academics children should also be exposed to various creative activities, sports, music and dance, and whatever the children show interest. Those interests of children should be nurtured, supported well and prioritized.

Children should also be taught the value of compassion, peace and non-discrimination. Above all, children should be taught to remain happy in all circumstances and to achieve such mental hygiene. They should be taught spirituality and meditation from a very early stage for living a creative, happy, compassionate, peaceful and balanced life.

To raise children well, their confidence is required to be boosted. Children lose their confidence and self-esteem when they are criticized or scolded in front of others. We as parents should never scold or criticize our kids in front of others and in case we need to scold or criticise them we should do it in private and we should also let the kids know the reason for it. As a saying goes, *'appreciate in public and criticize in private'*, so we, as parents, have to follow this adage in its letter and spirit.

The emphasis must be to mend their bad habits and patterns, and not to shun them in such a way that they lose their confidence and self-esteem. We have to communicate in a way that the message should be that they are not bad and do not lack anything, but their actions are not good and/or they have omitted to do certain things.

Avoid saying negative statements to the kids. We should avoid using the words 'don't', 'can't' etc and instead, we should use positive and encouraging words. Their energies should be channelized in a positive manner by letting them find their true interests and what they are naturally good at. We can only excel in the things we love and not in the things we do not like. Hence, our endeavour as parents should be to identify the God-gifted and natural talents in our kids because they can excel only in the pursuits which are their inherent and natural talents.

Children should also be given plenty of exposure to various cultures. We should take them to various places. Well-travelled children who have lived with people of multiple cultures having different colour, caste and creed are more accepting, grow well, adapt well and feel happy no matter where they go or with whom they live because it will help them understand people well and know how to easily mix-up with people of different cultures.

This is the time when we need to change our orthodox concepts of success, happiness and life, and must come out of the old thinking that only professional and successful people are Doctors, Engineers, MBAs etc. Let us look at the reality to understand if these people are the only ones who are really happy and successful. We need to give enough space to our kids to make career choices as per their interests and inherent talents.

Last but not the least, we should endeavour to raise children joyfully because what we all wish for our kids is success and happiness in the future but what about the present? Is the present not important? If parents and kids are not joyful and happy in the present, then what is the assurance that they will be happy and joyful in the future? Let us contemplate and raise our kids joyfully as their true selves, who will know their uniqueness and talents, and by doing so, they will become truly happy and successful grown-ups. We should also start implementing in our lives what we expect from our children and try to lead by example because children do not follow what is said but follow what they see. Ultimately, parenting is not just about raising children, it is about raising parents.

Section E

Let us be Spiritual beings!

Sixteen

Find A Guru Within!

As per Verse 4.34 of the Bhagavad Gita, one should approach a bonafide spiritual master to learn the truth as the self-realized spiritual master can impart the knowledge because he has seen the truth, however, the question is: how to know who is a bonafide spiritual master?

To reach this juncture where we can actually know who is a bonafide spiritual master, we have to start our spiritual journey alone and on the path of self-realization when we gain knowledge by self-study and practice we shall start finding many bonafide spiritual Masters and Gurus, who will help us in our journey of self-realization and finding the truth. It is said, *'when the seeker is ready; the master appears'*.

Thus, the most important thing is to start the spiritual journey by becoming your own Guru first and then on the path many spiritual gurus and masters will come into your life to teach you different aspects of self-realization and steadfast your spiritual journey. The only requirement is your dedicated, consistent and patient approach.

Who was the Guru of Buddha? The Buddha got enlightenment under a tree of wisdom. So, in the case of the Buddha, the wisdom tree was the Guru. So why not in your journey of self-realization, you should also find a tree of wisdom and make it one of your Gurus. When you sit under a tree and meditate, it will give you its energy because trees are the most awake living beings on Earth. In Upanishads, trees are said to be the incarnation of Shankar who takes in the poison (carbon dioxide) and gives out nectar (oxygen).

As Chanakya has said, *'religious austerities should be practiced alone'*. Hence, we have to start our spiritual practice alone, and with time, many great spiritual masters will appear and teach us different modes and make our spiritual practice strong and steady.

This is also important for us to know that Gurus can only initiate different wholesome seeds of self-realization and then, the journey is our own to find our own truth and have self-realization by watering these wholesome seeds. Different Gurus will give us different seeds in the form of their teachings: one Guru may teach us the art of meditation, mindfulness and living in the present moment; another may teach us a lesson of patience and serenity; other may teach us the lesson of compassion, peace and love; someone may teach us the art of relaxation; someone may teach us how to look for divinity within our own self; one can teach us how to dream meditatively; someone can teach us how to transcend the ego, how to let go and remove attachments and some can teach us a lesson of eternal bliss and happiness. So, when we can have many gurus to teach us many things, then, why stick ourselves to one person?

As venerable Dr Ajay Kotwal, an enlightened mystic and a Guru of Gurus says, *'when you have the fortune and luxury to take refuge and blessing from so many Gurus and all the God/Goddess of this cosmos, then, why should you follow and stick yourself to a single Guru'*. He says, *'learn from all of them and make all of the known and unknown Gurus part of your spiritual journey towards self-realization.'*

Also, a true Guru will ignite a Guru within you. As said by venerable Thich Nhat Hanh, Eminent Zen Master and Father of Mindfulness, *'A true teacher, a true spiritual partner, is one who encourages you to look deeply in yourself for the beauty and love you are seeking. The true teacher is someone who helps you discover the teacher in yourself'*.

It is also important to note that any spiritual practice to know the truth or your true self will never include dogmas and/or superstitions as for one who has realized the truth, he will never believe in any kind of superstitions and/or dogmas. Also, self-realized souls do not discriminate between good or bad, pure or impure, complete or incomplete and pious or impious, as for them, everything is created by the Supreme and everything is fine and anything is okay which comes on its own accord and they are away from all kind of dualities.

Verse 2.45 of the Bhagavad Gita provides that, *'The Vedas deal mainly with the subject of three modes of material nature. O Arjuna, become transcendental to these three modes. Be free from all dualities and from all anxieties for gain and safety, and be established in the self.'* In view thereof, a true transcendentalist has to go beyond the three modes of material nature that are a) Sattvam (Goodness); b) Rajah (Passion) and c) Tamah (Ignorance). If a Guru is preaching and believes in dogmas and/or superstitions, then, we need to open our eyes to his reality and see if he/she is a true Guru.

If you really want to look out for a teacher or Guru, then, you need to look for the transcendental qualities which are enumerated in Verse 16.1-3 of the Bhagavad Gita which are as follows:

16.1-3 *'The Supreme Personality of Godhead said, Fearlessness; purification of one's existence; cultivation of spiritual knowledge; charity; self-control; performance of sacrifice; study of the Vedas; austerity; simplicity; nonviolence; truthfulness; freedom from anger; renunciation; tranquillity; aversion to fault finding; compassion for all living entities; freedom from covetousness; gentleness; modesty; steady determination; vigour; forgiveness; fortitude; cleanliness; and freedom from envy and from the passion of honour - these transcendental qualities, O Son of Bharata, belong to the Godly men endowed with divine nature.'*

In view of the aforesaid, the True Guru or Bonafide Spiritual Master will be someone who has gone beyond all kinds of dualities and has the aforesaid transcendental qualities; may be not all but most of them; because, self-realization is a journey and even the Guru has to keep learning throughout his life to imbibe all of these qualities. Therefore, till the time, we find a Ture Guru or a Bonafide Spiritual Master let us start our spiritual journey on our own and find a Guru within to imbibe the transcendental qualities.

Practise:

Find a tree and sit under it for 15 to 30 minutes and try to breathe mindfully.

Seventeen

Spirituality in its true essence!

Is it important to become an ordained monk or sannyasi to tread on the path of spirituality or Sannyasa? Let us understand what is Sannyasa as per Bhagavad Gita. Verse 18.3 of the Bhagavad Gita provides as follows:

'The giving up of activities that are based on material desire is what great learned men call the renounced order of life (Sannyasa). And giving up the results of all activities is what the wise call renunciation (tyaga)'.

As per the above verse, leaving one's family and going to a secluded place or joining a formal sannyasi organization is not what Sannyasa means. What it truly means is giving up activities that are based on material desires.

The Buddha has said, *'One is forever on the way, yet has never left home. Another has left home, yet is not on the Way. Which one deserves to receive the offerings of humans and devas?*

Hence, we are not required to leave our homes and go to some solitary mountain or join some formal spiritual organization or ashram to be a Sannyasi or Spiritual. Spirituality is to know our true selves, to transcend all dualities and reaching a state of equanimity. It is to establish a connection with our soul/spirit. Hence, we can be spiritual or sannyasi where we are and do not need to go anywhere.

We should not fall into the trap of one-sidedness, which means we should never think that to be spiritual we have to leave our family, occupations and other things. Spirituality is coming home to yourself and not going somewhere else and getting lost. Just be where you are and practice spirituality. That is what the message of all the Buddhas is: to be what you are and living a life that is balanced and not one-sided. It has been aptly said by the Buddha, '*One is on a solitary peak and is unable to tread the path. Another one is at a busy crossroads yet is free from preferences. Which one is ahead, which one is behind?*'

Therefore, it is not necessary to leave everything and become an ordained monk or sannyasi to tread on the path of spirituality. We can be spiritual just by being lay practitioners. Only requirement is to find a suitable path or Yoga.

In the Bhagavad Gita, there are three types of spiritual practices or Yoga on which human beings can tread and they are Karma Yoga, Bhakti Yoga and Dhyana Yoga. To follow a path, yoga, practice which is best suited to you, initially, you may need to tread on all the paths and find out yourself which one is best suited to you. For instance, Meera Bhai followed the path of Bhakti Yoga, Buddha followed the path of Dhyana Yoga and Raja Janak followed the path of Karma Yoga. For the purpose of this chapter, we are focusing on Dhyana Yoga which is considered to be the highest form of Yoga.

Now, let us also understand what do Yoga and the Yogi mean? It would be helpful to produce herein what Venerable Sri Sri Paramahansa Yogananda has written about Yoga in his book The Autobiography of a Yogi while reiterating the words of Dr CG Jung, 'Every religious or philosophical practice means a psychological discipline, that is, a method of mental hygiene. The manifold, purely bodily procedure of Yoga also means mental hygiene which is superior to ordinary gymnastics and breathing exercises.'

Therefore, what Yoga means is a psychological discipline and that is to upkeep mental hygiene and spirituality or yoga is actually to upkeep our mental hygiene, which is why it is beyond our physical bodies. Our physical bodies are meant to deteriorate and end with time, however, if taken care of, the mind has a nature to grow and go beyond our physical bodies. As it is said that mind and/or consciousness is as old as the Universe, so taking care of the mind and consciousness is taking care of life beyond our present bodily manifestation. Verse 6.18 of the Bhagavad Gita provides as follows:

'When the yogi, by practice of yoga, disciplines his mental activities and becomes situated in transcendence devoid of all material desires-he is said to be well established in yoga.'

Do whatever you want to do but try to establish yourself in Spirituality or Yoga and that is the highest purpose of our lives, and to establish ourselves in Yoga or Spirituality or Sannyasa, we have to go beyond the concept that, we have to leave our present circumstances, our home, occupation, family and friends, on the other hand, if spiritual discipline or yoga practices are followed properly, it will bring us closer to our family, friends, relatives, occupation and worldly affairs because following a spiritual practice or yoga is taking care of our mind, which is being totally ignored by laypeople like us thinking that if we follow spirituality or sannyasa or Adyatam, we have to leave our current circumstances, our homes and families. That is a narrow approach and it is also called spiritual escapism.

On the other hand, if we follow a spiritual or yoga practice, it will show us a path where we can have meaningful relationships, we become peaceful and truly happy individuals just by being where we are. Such is the path of Right Mindfulness or Dhyana Yoga. It connects you to your inner self, which gives you the courage to offload the societal conditioning, become your true self, live fearlessly, reach a state of equanimity and enjoy yourself and your loved ones.

Spirituality is wonderful and sannyasa is really meaningful because it just means that we have to give up the activities that are based on material desire, and every weekend at least, we can take an opportunity to try giving up the activities that are based on material desires to have the taste of Sannyasa and Yoga. Most of our activities are based on fear of achieving and losing materialistic things, which creates constant fear, and fear creates delusion, unwarranted actions and the result is desperation.

Once we are able to tread on the path of spirituality, we will see the reality, and the first reality is that we are merely puppets in the hands of an ultimate power who is creating, planning and executing everything seamlessly and in abundance. Look around you and see, how this power plans the sunset and sunrise; phases of the moon; growing trees and the jungles; blooming the buds into flowers; ripening the fruits and vegetables; feeding the birds and animals and; scheduling birth and death which is taking place in each and every moment.

When you will have this understanding, you will automatically give up activities that are based on material desires and come out of the mistaken belief that you are the doer, and then you will place the thread of your life in the hand of that Ultimate Power who is planning and creating wonders, miracles and abundance; and you will start taking actions without worrying about the fruits of those actions and as a call of your higher duty and unique purpose which is a sure sign of an extraordinary and blissful life beyond all kind of miseries. That is what happens when we truly walk on the path of Sannyasa and become a true Sannyasi and a Yogi. Verse 6.46 of the Bhagavad Gita provides that *'A Yogi is greater than the ascetic, greater than the empiricist and greater than the fruitive worker, therefore, O Arjuna, in all circumstances, be a Yogi'.*

Eighteen

Peaceful Mind for Peaceful world

When we see a picture of the Buddha, we see him sitting with crossed legs and meditating. Yes, Buddha has given us meditation. Buddha has given us tools for concentration and by developing concentration, we can attain insight and when we have insight, our understanding increases, and with the power of understanding, we can create love and by creating love, shall we not solve all our problems in life, such as, have better relationships, increase productivity, peace in society and the world and as a result, awesome quality of life, full of peace and happiness.

What is meditation? Meditation is giving ourselves our true presence. Are we present and available to us? Most of the time, we are lost in the past and in the future. The Buddha has said, *'Past is gone and the future is not yet here, present is the only moment available to us.'* We actually create the present moment, a passing moment or gap between the past and the future, and we, actually, do not live our life which is only available in the present moment.

Buddha after getting enlightenment shared his teachings. If we really try to learn and understand the teachings of the Buddha, we will realize that the whole message of Buddha is that we do not have to go anywhere for enlightenment or nirvana, enlightenment and nirvana are available in the here and now. Eminent Zen Master Thich Nath Hanh has said *'there is no enlightenment outside of daily life.'*

The teachings of Buddha are very simple. He has made Dhyana Yoga very easy and simple. If we see the life of Buddha and the way he led his life, we will understand that Buddha has exactly done what is written in Chapter 6 of Bhagavad Gita titled as Dhyana Yoga, and the Buddha has practiced Dhyana Yoga in its letter and spirit and after practicing and getting enlightenment, Buddha's realization and teaching is that we do not need to go anywhere for enlightenment, we can be enlightened where we are and by living our normal lives. It is not important to become a monastic to follow the teachings of Buddha and even by being a lay practitioner, we can practice the teachings of Buddha and attain enlightenment. That is what Buddha has given; to realize our true selves or gain enlightenment by living where we are merely by using various forms of Dhyana Yoga.

The Buddha has given three forms of Dhyana or meditation which are as follows:

1) Meditation/Samadhi in stillness: This is sitting meditation wherein we sit crossed legs and concentrate our mind by observing our breath or any other object and we lay down in stillness and

do total relaxation by scanning our body parts, this is the same practice as yoga nidra.

2) Meditation/Samadhi in motion: This meditation includes meditation or developing concentration and awareness in every activity we perform while walking we can do walking meditation, while eating we can do eating meditation, while reading we go do reading meditation etc. We only need to create concentration and awareness in each and every activity we perform.

3) Meditation/Samadhi in observing our surroundings: This meditation provides that when we cannot do either meditation in stillness or meditation in motion, we can do meditation in observing our surroundings. Suppose, we are sitting somewhere or sitting in a bus, car etc and we cannot do both the aforesaid meditations, then, we start observing our surroundings such as we use our senses to see what is happening, we can look at the sky, the sun, moon, tree etc, we can hear the sounds of the birds, sounds near and far, sound of the air and sound of the silence. We can observe our breath and the quality of air going in and coming out, the things we can smell and the taste in the mouth and sensation and/or feeling on our skin or body.

The whole message of Buddha after enlightenment was to follow the Noble Eightfold path which are 1) Right View; 2) Right Resolve; 3) Right Speech; 4) Right Conduct; 5) Right Livelihood; 6) Right Effort; 7) Right Mindfulness; and 8) Right Concentration. The Buddha has given these eightfold paths with a view to transcend suffering into happiness because the four noble truths are: 1) that suffering exists; 2) there are reasons for suffering; 3) happiness also exists and; 4) there is a path to happiness.

Right mindfulness has been considered as one of the most excellent paths to happiness because once we become mindful which is also awareness, we can have concentration, and if we have the right concertation, we will have the right insight and once we have insight, we can create understanding and once we have the right understanding, our view, resolve, speech, conduct, livelihood and efforts shall become right. Hence, Buddha has given us the practice of mindfulness which is very easy. It starts from observing our breath to activities to thoughts and then converting our negative thoughts into positive thoughts which will help us take the right actions and the right action shall result in positivity in our life and ultimately, happiness.

Why are most of us unhappy despite having everything we need and desired at some point in time? Because we are lost in our desires and desires have become a continuous process. We have never-ending desires like the desire to have more money, power, fame etc and most of these desires are either to compete with each other and/or to show off. Until the time we are driven by these desires and keep running after them, we will not be able to attain real peace and love and will also not be able to eliminate hate and violence. Buddha's teaching does not say that we should not have desires but says, it is attachment to desires which makes us suffer. Let us desire without getting attached to it. To do this, we have to develop a habit to let go.

Because of running, competing, comparing etc we have not been able to develop the right insight and understanding. Our minds are loaded with thoughts and a continuous chatter is going on and on in our minds. And when there are so many thoughts going on in our mind, we lose our ability to see reality as it is and become calm and peaceful which are basic ingredients for true happiness. We often confuse happiness with excitement but as per Buddha true happiness is based on serenity, calmness, composure, equanimity and peacefulness.

Our minds are like mirrors that get dirty by various types of consumption. We consume by different modes: by eyes, we consume what we see; by ears, we consume what we hear; by the mouth, we consume what we eat and what we converse, and by the nose, we consume what we smell and by touch we consume what we feel. Hence, if we have to improve our life, the Buddha has said that we should be mindful of what we are consuming because by being mindful of our consumption, we can influence our mind. Buddha has said, *'Mind is everything, what we think we become.'*

Buddha has given a message to the world that peace is very important and peace is the only way to resolve all our disputes, and peace is possible and peace is available within us, it only needs practice, and mindfulness is the practice to attain peace. Peace is the only way, peace in mind will create peace in the world.

Let us try to walk a little on the path given by Buddha which is creating peace within us, our families, our societies, our communities, our city, our state, our country and in the world. Let us create a world that is peaceful. The latest pandemic of COVID-19 has shown us that all the world is one and we are inter-are with each other. We all are human beings and the border cannot divide us physically as we are made up of the same particles. Let us start creating this peaceful world by working on ourselves first because it is said that charity begins from home and we are our true home. Let us meditate to make ourselves peaceful and if everybody tries to become peaceful, the world will become peaceful. The Dalai Lama has said, '*if every 8-year-old in the world is taught meditation, we will eliminate violence from the world within one generation*'.

Section F

Let us meditate!

Nineteen

Breath is the God within.

In all religions, breath is considered to be the God within. Relevant verses of various sacred texts are given below:

The Bhagavad Gita in Verse 10.22 provides that *'of the Vedas I am the Sāma Veda; of the demigods I am Indra, the king of heaven; of the senses I am the mind; and in living beings I am the living force (breath)'.*

The Quran in Verse 15:28 provides that '*When your Lord said to the angels, I will create the human being out of pure mud-moulded clay' and* Verse 15:29 provides that *'when I have made him complete and breathed into him of My spirit, fall down making obeisance to him'* and this is again repeated in Verse 38:72 of the Quran.

The Holy Bible in Genesis 2.7 provides that *'then the Lord God formed the man of dust from the ground and breathed into his nostrils the breath of life and the man become the living creature'.*

As such, breath is a God within and breathing right and in awareness is equivalent to remembering God. Right breathing will also enhance the quality and longevity of life. Awareness of breath is also a halter of thoughts because having a lot of thoughts is the major reason for mental and physical health issues.

Also, many illustrations could be given on the relationship between a man's respiratory rate and the variations in his states of consciousness or health. Quick or uneven breaths are an inevitable accompaniment of harmful emotional states: fear, lust, anger. The restless monkey breathes at the rate of 32 times a minute, in contrast to a man's average of 18 times. The elephant, tortoise, snake, and other creatures noted for their longevity have a respiratory rate that is less than man's. The giant tortoise, for instance, which may attain the age of three hundred years, breathes only 4 times a minute.

Breathing well helps us in keeping healthy oxygen levels as breath is the only source of oxygen for the body, hence, it becomes imperative to breathe properly especially during this epidemic as people suffering from Corona are not able to maintain saturation of oxygen levels. The reason for not maintaining healthy oxygen levels is not breathing right. Most of the time, we breathe till nose, throat or chest which do not supply sufficient oxygen to vital organs of the body, hence, our oxygen levels go down and we need more oxygen than needed to stay healthy and fit, both, physically and mentally.

Breath is also a bridge between our body and mind. When we breathe in awareness, we come back to the present moment. Our body and mind get aligned and as we are in the present moment, our thoughts reduce manifold and as we have less or no thoughts we become calm, composed and peaceful. There are ways to breathe well and there are yogic techniques that are very helpful.

Below are a few breathing exercises and techniques which can be the starting point of your spiritual journey and life of equanimity which is beyond happiness and sorrow:

1. Be mindful of your posture, time and again erect your spine. Keeping the spine straight and erect helps in better breathing and circulation of breath in the torso and vital organs. Put a reminder of some kind, such as the sound of a bell. A bell of mindfulness or the sound of Tibetan gong/singing bowl as a ring tone of a phone can be helpful.

2. Do diaphragm breathing. Pay attention to your diaphragm, a muscular sheet between your chest and stomach. When you breathe in, particularly with deep breaths from your diaphragm, your abdomen rises. When you breathe out, your diaphragm pushes air out and your abdomen falls. Also, you need to manipulate your out-breaths a little by making them slower. The out-breath should be longer than the in-breath. Time and again bring your attention to your abdomen and observe the rise and fall of your abdomen, and say inside your mind, 'rise' while breathing in, and 'fall' while breathing out. Diaphragm breathing will help in reducing the need for oxygen in the body and with less oxygen, appropriate levels of oxygen can be maintained. Again, put a reminder of some kind for doing diaphragm breathing or club it with the straightening of the spine. Reduce the number of times of in- and out-breaths to 8 to 10 breaths in a minute.

3. Many times, take a deep breath and hold it inside as long as possible and then, release and make sure that your out-breath is longer than the in-breath to help release more carbon dioxide from the body. If you are disturbed, worried, tensioned or thinking a lot, then, take the help of diaphragm breathing, observe the rise and fall of your abdomen and bring your awareness to your feet and feel the sensations at the sole of your feet. Increase the duration of each breath every time you hold it inside.

4. Body scan, a popular practice in yoga, mindfulness and in clinics for stress and pain. This is a simple practice that will help you become more aware of your body and relax and heal your body. The body scan can be done standing or sitting, but the best is done lying down. Very slowly let your awareness and attention move through your body, beginning at the head and moving to the sole of your feet or vice-versa and one possible sequence through your body would be starting from the head to forehead to eyes to nose to lips to neck to shoulders to arms to hands to chest to diaphragm to abdomen/navel to pelvis to legs to toes to the sole of the feet and when bringing your awareness to the body parts, while inhaling say, 'I am aware of my head, eyes', and while exhaling say, 'I calm and relax my head, eyes', etc. Do a body scan at least once a day, it will help to relax your body and mind, and a relaxed being needs less oxygen.

Last but not the least, breathe mindfully as breath is God within all of us. So, let us find God within and in others. Let us also honour each other and live a life of brotherhood and sisterhood because there is no religion above brotherhood and sisterhood.

Twenty

Meditation in Stillness

Mindfulness meditation is the alignment of body and mind. It is to bring your mind back to your body and enjoying the present moment. The main ingredient of mindfulness meditation is breath. The purpose of mediation is to silent the continuous chattering going on inside our minds. The outer world can never be silent. Silence is internal. Our mind is silent when it does not have internal chatter and because there is no chatter inside the mind, we can focus and concentrate even in the busy crossroads full of external noises. This is what meditation does, it silences the chatter of our mind and our mind becomes calm and peaceful. God resides in a silent mind and when our mind is silent nothing external can disturb or irritate us.

The Technique of mindfulness meditation is given below:

If possible, light an incense, and wash your face, hands and feet. Please note, you can do it at any time as per your convenience.

You can sit cross-legged on a floor or on a chair or while traveling in a car (chauffeur-driven), bus, train, or plane.

Keep your spine straight. Use a cushion to sit and put it under your hips. It will help in keeping the spine straight.

Hold your hands together by crossing your fingers, and place the right thumb on the left thumb.

Look at the tip of your nose, and then close your eyes slowly, and you can say the following inside your mind while meditating:

S.No.	While inhaling say	While exhaling say
1	In	Out
2	Deep	Slow
3	Calm	Ease
4	Smile	Release
5	Present moment	Wonderful moment

Please try to implement the meaning of each word in its letter and spirit. Saying it inside your mind is very important.

While doing the in and out at serial no. 1, just become aware of your in- and out-breath and let it be natural. You just need to be aware of the same. In this exercise, time and again bring your attention to your nostrils and observe the air coming in and going out. The air coming in will be cool and the air going out will be warm. Keep doing it, till the time your breath naturally gets deeper.

When doing the deep and slow at serial no. 2, try to do the diaphragm breathing. Here you need to manipulate your out-breaths a little by making it slower. Your out-breath should be longer than you're in-breath. Time and again bring your attention to your abdomen and observe the rise and fall of your abdomen, and say inside your mind 'rise' while breathing in, and 'fall' while breathing out.

When you deeply inhale and slowly exhale, you become calm and when you become calm, things become easy. While inhaling, you have to say, 'calm', and while exhaling, you have to say, 'ease'. While saying calm, really calm yourself by releasing the stiffness in your body, and while saying ease, just give half a smile intentionally. Repeat it till the time you really feel calm.

When you become calm and things become easy, you smile and when you smile, you relax three hundred muscles on your face and you also release the tension in your body. While inhaling say 'smile' and smile a bit and while exhaling say 'release' and bring your attention to the sole of your feet and feel the sensations there and imagine that all the tension, worries, fears, frustration etc are getting released from there, and when negative thoughts are released, the present moment becomes a wonderful moment.

Now, while inhaling say, 'present moment', and while exhaling say, 'wonderful moment'. This is a very important exercise and while doing this, bring your awareness to the sense organs one by one and try to hear all the sounds near and far, try to see images while your eyes are closed, try to have the taste in your mouth, try to smell the fragrance and the quality of air coming in and going out and then at last try to feel the sensations on your skin.

You may meditate for 15 minutes to half an hour or more. In case you need any clarification, you may get in touch with us.

In addition to this, please also note that while meditating, we can breathe in many forms. We start with following our natural breath, then, we may manipulate our breath a little by taking a long breath and exhaling slowly. Sometimes, we become aware of the gap in two breaths. Sometimes, we hold our breath after taking an in-breath and we pause after taking an out-breath. So, we change the pattern of our breaths as per the need. Deep breath is taken from the diaphragm and we observe the rise and fall of our abdomen. It is called diaphragm breathing. Sometimes, we just become aware of our natural breathing and focus on the tip of our nose or nostrils.

Sometimes, we take a deep breath and hold it inside as long as possible and exhale and keep our lungs empty as long as possible. It depends upon different situations and conditions of our mind. If you are disturbed, worried, tense or thinking a lot, then, take the help of diaphragm breathing, observe the rise and fall of your abdomen and bring your awareness to your feet and feel the sensations there. When your mind is not much disturbed and/or agitated, observe the breath at your nostrils. If you need to energize yourself, pause after you breathe out and if you need to calm yourself, hold your breath after breathing in.

Taste the nectar of mindfulness meditation and feel the calm bliss, and once you have tasted this nectar, you will like to taste it time and again to become calm, composed and blissful.

Twenty-one

Meditation in Motion

Meditation in motion includes walking meditation, eating meditation, driving meditation, drinking meditation etc. Meditation in motion is becoming mindful/aware/conscious of each and every activity of the day from our waking till the time we sleep. Every activity is an opportunity for meditation. When we walk and concentrate on our steps, it becomes meditation. When we are eating and are fully aware and concentrate on eating, it becomes meditation. So, each and every activity performed in the light of awareness and concentration becomes meditation. Techniques of various meditations are given below:

1) Walking Meditation: Before starting to walk, just stand and take three deep breaths and then start walking very slowly and match your steps with your breath. One step, one in-breath and another step, one out-breath and you can also speak in your mind in or out or any other word you feel is right. So, it is the coordination of three things: step, breath and speech.

2) Eating Meditation: Before starting eating. Take three breaths. Look at the food. Observe the texture

of the food and say inside your mind while breathing in, 'Thank you universe for giving me this wholesome food,' and while breathing out, 'May I eat this food in mindfulness so as to be worthy to have received this food.' Food that comes on our plate is a gift from the Universe. Every time we eat our food, try to go into the history of the food, and you would see that the whole universe has worked to get you this food from the cook to the farmer to nature. The entire universe has worked for us to give us this food and we often take the food for granted and eat it either in hurry or in forgetfulness. We should also never waste our food as wasting it is an insult to the whole cosmos.

3) Drinking meditation: Drink your tea, water or any other thing in mindfulness and concentration. These all are gifts from the entire cosmos and apply the same steps as given in eating meditation. Aside, just hold the cup or glass in your hand and feel the sensation of the cup or glass.

4) Reading or writing meditation: Whenever you read or write, just read a line with one in-breath and another line in the out-breath. If you are not able to concentrate, take a deep breath, hold it inside for some time and release the breath slowly. Your concentration shall increase manifold and reading and writing will become meditation.

5) Driving or Riding meditation: Whenever you drive your car or ride your motorcycle or cycle. Before starting, take three deep breaths. While driving or riding when you are changing the gear or accelerating, match these actions with your breath. For example, when you press the clutch, inhale and

when releasing, exhale. Do not take for granted driving or riding as that is the biggest reason for accidents because most of the time, our body is driving but our mind is thinking something else and hence, our body and mind are not aligned and we are not fully attentive or aware while driving the car or riding our motor or bicycle.

6) Telephone meditation: Whenever you call someone or someone calls you, before giving or taking the call, take three breaths and then talk to the person on the other side. This way you will become mindful of your talk and will be there with the person on call. By breathing mindfully, we call our mind back to our body which may be busy in the past or the future.

7) Smiling Meditation: Just smile and do smiling meditation. While breathing in say, 'I calm my body and mind', and while breathing out say, 'I smile' and smile a bit. It is said that sometimes joy is the source of our smile and sometimes, a smile is the source of joy. Hence, smile because smiling is a face yoga, it relaxes the muscles of your face and it shows that you are in control of your mind.

8) Tree Hugging Meditation: Tree hugging meditations are also a very effective kind of meditation. When we hug a tree, we take the calmness and peacefulness of a tree. People may call you mad for hugging a tree but tree hugging meditation is a blessing.

9) Tea Meditation

a) Look at your tea for some time and see the texture and colour of the tea and also try to find in the cup of your tea the sunshine, the cloud, the soil, the farmer, the retailer, the person who has made the tea etc because if you mindfully observe, you will get an insight that entire cosmos/universe is there in the cup of your tea.

b) Breathe in and out three times and while breathing say inside your mind, 'May I drink this tea in mindfulness and with concentration so as to be worthy to have this cup of tea as this tea is a gift from the cosmos/universe'.

c) Then, slowly and mindfully raise the cup of your tea to your mouth and drink it slowly by tasting and relishing each and every sip in your mouth for a few seconds.

d) In the gaps between the sips, mindfully breathe in and out and also mindfully observe your surroundings.

Twenty-two

Meditation of Observing Surroundings

The meditation of observing surroundings can be done where and when we cannot either do meditation in stillness or in motion, such as, while sitting in a bus, or waiting for our turn or just sitting in a garden or somewhere but we cannot do either of the aforesaid meditations. The meditation of observing surroundings includes 1) listening to the chirping of the birds, sounds near and far and sound of the air; 2) watching a tree and listening to the sound of the air passing through the leaves of the tree; 3) seeing the sunlight through the leaves of the tree; 4) smiling at strangers; 5) trying to smell everything we can; 6) observing the quality of air coming in and going out form the nostrils; 7) trying to feel the taste we have in the mouth; and 8) feeling the things that touch our skin such as the cool breeze that touches our face and body or body parts touching each other and/or body touching other things.

These are the meditations wherein we use our senses to come back to the present moment and become aware and mindful.

Some short meditations and practises:

1) Be aware of the gap between two breaths.

2) Deeply inhale and slowly exhale three times.

3) Look at the tip of your nose and breathe mindfully thrice.

4) Listen to the chirping of the birds.

5) Consider setting the ringtone of your phone as a bell of mindfulness and whenever it rings, breathe mindfully.

6) Take the breath and hold the breath for some time and release the breath and pause for some time.

7) Listen to some soothing music and feel it within you.

8) Light an incense stick and become aware of its fragrance.

9) Look at a flower for some time and mindfully smell the fragrance of the flower.

10) Hug a tree considering it to be a living being or your friend.

11) Press your eyes with your index fingers and try to see the light in between your eyebrows.

12) Continuously look at your shadow for a minute or two.

13) Drink water and have the taste of it. Visualize the place of its origin.

14) Look at something without blinking for half a minute (any light, a bulb, moon or sun) and then close your eyes and try to see the light or image of these in between your eyebrows (third eye).

15) Perform Shanmukhi Mudra: index and middle fingers close the eyes, thumbs close the ear by pressing the ear flaps against the ear opening, the ring fingers close the nostrils and little fingers at the two ends of the lips. Take a breath by removing only the index fingers from the nose and after taking a breath as per the requirement. Keep all the sense organs closed as long as you can and hold your breath in. Repeat it five to seven times. On every attempt try to see a light between your eyebrows and also listen to the sounds inside.

Now, you have awakened to a new world of pure consciousness, eternal bliss and true happiness. Stay awake!

www.ingramcontent.com/pod-product-compliance
Ingram Content Group UK Ltd.
Pitfield, Milton Keynes, MK11 3LW, UK
UKHW041957190726
13854UKWH00005B/2030